YOUR KNOWLEDGE HAS

- We will publish your bachelor's and
  master's thesis, essays and papers

- Your own eBook and book -
  sold worldwide in all relevant shops

- Earn money with each sale

Upload your text at www.GRIN.com
and publish for free

Mathews George

Cloud Computing. Actionable Architecture

GRIN Publishing

Bibliographic information published by the German National Library:

The German National Library lists this publication in the National Bibliography; detailed bibliographic data are available on the Internet at http://dnb.dnb.de .

Imprint:

Copyright © 2011 GRIN Verlag, Open Publishing GmbH
Print and binding: Books on Demand GmbH, Norderstedt Germany
ISBN: 978-3-656-58084-3

This book at GRIN:

http://www.grin.com/en/e-book/262815/cloud-computing-actionable-architecture

GRIN - Your knowledge has value

Since its foundation in 1998, GRIN has specialized in publishing academic texts by students, college teachers and other academics as e-book and printed book. The website www.grin.com is an ideal platform for presenting term papers, final papers, scientific essays, dissertations and specialist books.

Visit us on the internet:

http://www.grin.com/

http://www.facebook.com/grincom

http://www.twitter.com/grin_com

Cloud Computing – Actionable Architecture

- Dr. Mathews K. George

  [P.D.F., Ph.D. (FE), Ph.D. (CS), M.S. (FE), M.S. (AM), M.B.A., B.S. (ASE).]

ABSTRACT

This paper will demonstrate a pragmatic methodology, used in conjunction with UML (unified modeling language), BPMN (business process modeling notation) along with engineering principles for describing an actionable architecture for cloud computing in the real world. The fundamental paradigm of cloud computing, whether it is for private or public usage, revolves around the provisioning of services for everyone through rich resources that can be synergized through Internet-based protocols.

The true definition of Cloud Computing is, according to the author, all about the practicalities of "outsourcing" all aspects of using computing resources to some form of external "agency". This means that the assumption for any cloud computing usage is the fact that the "agency" has a powerful resource base (hardware, software, infrastructure, platforms, power supply, backups, failover mechanisms as well as management skills). Therefore, all users of the cloud computing services provided by the "agency" can work in a well-defined "demand-supply" mode, with an insurmountable base of possible fault-tolerant mechanisms to support best possible user experiences. The user will have the unique experience of not being worried about where his/her work is being done because cloud computing, as defined above, will enable him/her to work in a "virtualized" environment but with the feeling of being close to the resources.

However, the apparent ease available through cloud computing will raise problems associated with diverse types of risks. Hence, it is imperative to define new architectural blueprints as well as the associated business processes around them so as to provide measurable metrics that will allay the fears of any user. The architectural blueprint is not just meant to be a lot of diagrams and documents but they are to be modeled as actionable artifacts. These actionable artifacts will allow for operational excellence that covers all types of functional as well as non-functional requirements that any user expects. The MDA (model driven architecture) approach, coupled with BPM (business process modeling) and engineering principles, as posited in this paper, will allow for management of distributed communication, scheduling, security enhancements and rights (as well as many other aspects) that will make the user experience enjoyable and successful.

COPYRIGHT AND LEGAL NOTICES
WITH APPLICABLE DISCLAIMERS

Table of Contents

1. INTRODUCTION 4
   1.1 PURPOSE...4
   1.2 BUSINESS DRIVERS..5
2. APPROACH...6
   2.1 CSB (CLOUD SERVICE BUS) – FORMALISM..6
   2.2 BPM 7
   2.3 USE CASE MODEL (REQUIREMENTS)..7
   2.4 SEQUENCE MODEL (SCENARIOS)...9
   2.5 COMPONENT MODEL...10
   2.6 DEPLOYMENT MODEL...11
   2.7 CSB MODEL DRIVEN ARCHITECTURE...12
3. CONCLUSION 13
4. REFERENCES 14
5. CITATIONS..14
6. ACKNOWLEDGEMENTS 14

1. Introduction

1.1 Purpose

There are many types of ideas and purported cloud computing implementations that are available today. Many leading vendors and providers have "outsourcing" models that currently support private as well as public cloud computing infrastructure. Examples of PaaS (platform as a service), SaaS (software as a service), IaaS (infrastructure as a service) and the like abound today. Leaders in this whole space (AT&T, IBM, Oracle, Microsoft, HP, Amazon as well as other smaller companies) are in the cloud computing space. However, it is clear that the missing dimension is one that can cover user requirements in such a manner that an actionable computing architecture can be created so as to drive the real-world implementation of this type of service offering.

An excellent paper published by K. Mukherjee and G. Sahoo [Reference 1], in the 2009 IEEE "International Conference on Advances in Computing, Control and Telecommunication Technologies", has provided a great deal of insight into the mathematical modeling framework vis-à-vis cloud computing as a whole. This excellent paper explains, in a very lucid manner, all the details of what the agenda of cloud computing is, along with details of runtime entities involved in cloud computing, as per the practical needs of users who pay for the services on a "pay-per-usage" or "dedicated basis".

The other set of great work has been done by Joe Weinman of AT&T [Reference 2] who has put forth multifarious papers and discussion blogs that point to the business value of cloud computing. He has described and proved many aspects of how cloud computing will work with the present backbone infrastructure already available (through telecommunications companies/providers) and what it means to migrate to such an environment. Joe Weinman has compared all his mathematical proofs, business value propositions and recommendations based on the fundamental model of a "utility company model". He has published so many great papers that explain cost factors, peaks, demands and how to optimize cloud computing for all types of users depending on their needs. Joe Weinman has done seminal work on topics covering "Mathematical Proof of the Inevitability of Cloud Computing", "Cloudonomics", "Hybrid Cloud" and "Virtual Private Cloud", all of which present the pellucid models of working with cloud computing independent of which vendor is involved.

It is also worth mentioning, at this juncture, that I [the author of this Infosys paper (Dr. Mathews K. George)] have derived wonderful inspiration provided by all the works of Peter Fingar (the ultimate guru of BPM – business process management – among other things) in the discipline of cloud computing. Peter Fingar has published a book called "Enterprise Cloud Computing" [Reference 3] as well as a seminal paper called "Fractal Enterprise Architecture and Agent-Oriented BPM: Can UML or BPMN Model a Cloud?" from which some ideas for this paper have been taken.

Some examples of true cloud computing implementations for lay persons (users) are the Turbo Tax, Sales Force and Amazon web sites as well as their backend systems in their respective clouds. In more ways than one can imagine, these pioneering companies have been providing utility-like services for any user and everything is based on a cloud computing agenda.

Sun Microsystems was one of the pioneers in envisioning the "network as the computer" paradigm and they had come up with actionable architecture models for cloud computing as one of the first in the race.

I [the author of the current paper] have used many of the fundamental ideas from Sun's seminal work without focusing on proprietary technologies but more on open-source platforms.

With the above referenced inspirations, and borrowing ideas from 3 models [Reference 4, Reference 5, Reference 6], I [the author of this paper] have ventured onto an attempt to capture an actionable architectural model for cloud computing by demonstrating the abstract steps needed. This approach will show how to map the user requirements (use cases) and business processes to specific artifacts that will form the architecture of cloud computing in the real world.

The purpose of my paper is to justify that "Cloud Computing" is a metaphor for the Internet/Web. As stated by all the experts (alluded to in the references), "Cloud Computing" is all about accessibility of platforms, infrastructure, software, applications, systems and the like for satisfying the needs of users and to enable them to work in a virtualized environment. This implies that everything they (the users) need will be driven from the physical CSB (cloud service bus) which contains a mixture of hardware, firmware, software, data, storage, power grids and the like to keep all systems running efficiently with full "fault-tolerance".

In effect, the driving force behind my paper is to state that "Cloud Computing" and CSB manifest a type of "programmable model" wherein all resources are accessible through an "interface" as though the user is sitting just next to the source. All this is about new "programmable models", "programmable infrastructures" and the enabling of "programmable business models."

1.2 Business Drivers

It is currently upon all of us to realize the fact that enterprises are moving on to actionable CSB (cloud service bus) infrastructures. What this implies is that users will be enabled to do all routine work with minimal investment at home or office and will also be able to connect to a choice of any operating system, applications, storage, data, information flow and all types of hardware or firmware.

The very physical realities of traditional business processes are now ripe for change. This, according to Peter Fingar, means that the complex global enterprise goes beyond a flat plane. He states that fractal geometry principles provide a fresh foundation for business modeling and Enterprise Architecture. According to the works of Peter Fingar [Reference 3], any company is just a complex social system, a system that must be treated as such, a complex organism of many dimensions and components – customers, producers and suppliers (and their information systems) fused together as **one** to create **Value Networks**. The days of the vertically integrated or one-dimensional company are over. Linear value chains have morphed into complex, multi-dimensional business eco-systems that have a lifecycle that goes from "birth" to "optimization" and on to a "state of entropy" as do all systems in the universe. Hence, all cloud computing systems will follow an EA (Enterprise Architecture) model as well as new tenets of BPM (Business Processing Management) models to accommodate complex variations of demand-supply and the phenomenon of value networks will provide new dimensions as business drivers.

The core business driver of any enterprise vis-à-vis cloud computing revolves around 3 fundamental tenets – (1) interfaces, (2) information and (3) messages/services. These 3 dimensions are very crucial in all forms of communications amongst various applications or systems. Furthermore, CSB will also have to cover other aspects for the enterprise-wide needs like software, hardware, networks, systems, workflows and business processes (to name the most important).

The total value for any business will be judged by lower costs, higher qualities and total reliability of any service provided to users. This means that a CSB (cloud service bus) will be able to take care of IaaS, PaaS, SaaS or any other type of need that can be classified as a utility service for all types of users.

In summary, the following are some of the greatest business benefits vis-à-vis cloud computing.

- Business Agility – The infrastructure will be rapidly scalable for all types of users within the shortest possible time with horizontal as well as vertical scaling of all components.
- Efficiency – Virtualization will drive all operations and IT costs will drop down with high quality outputs for all users.
- Data Center costs will be driven down to the best levels and only operational efficiencies need to be accounted for.
- Capital Expenditure will be reduced.
- There will be no need to "over-provision" any type of service because everything can be scaled dynamically on parallel processing levels (massive scaling at rapid time intervals).
- All life cycles will become dynamically flexible and this includes hardware, firmware, software and everything that goes into making the infrastructure operational.

2. Approach

This paper will demonstrate a pragmatic methodology, used in conjunction with UML (unified modeling language), for describing CSB vis-à-vis cloud computing and businesses around it. The theme of this paper is centered on the abstraction of "Cloud Computing" as a CSB model with a focus on how to build an actionable architecture through MDA (model driven architecture) principles.

2.1 CSB (Cloud Service Bus) – Formalism

The formal model of a CSB allows a system to have other systems as inputs and outputs. Therefore, the system that accepts other systems as inputs can be considered a "**metasystem**" from the input systems context. There could be many layers of "metasystem and system" pairs. In this type of model for a CSB, systems engineering activities become the main focus in order to determine design considerations revolving around demand, supply, peak loads, mean and median (to name just a few salient parameters) on developing and deploying a utility-type set of services that form the foundation of cloud computing.

The following lists all the 6 requirements which are foundational to CSB.

- Input/output requirement
- Technology requirement
- Performance requirement
- Cost/financial requirement
- Trade-off requirement
- System test requirement

2.2 BPM

With the discussions on formalism, the next logical step is to show a BPM (Business Process Management) model of what is involved in CSB life cycles.

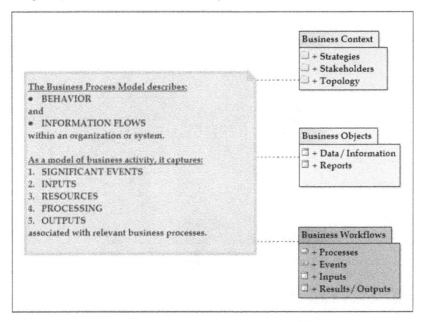

Figure 1: Business Process Model – Abstract View

The explanation of Figure 1 is given in the bullet points listed below. All the notations are provided by using UML which will help every stakeholder understand the problem to be solved and to communicate visually with minimal chances of ambiguity.

- The Business Context "package" contains models of all involved stakeholders, mission statements, business goals and physical structure of the business "as-is".
- The Business Objects "package" contains the domain model of all objects of interest and their respective data/information.
- The Business Workflows "package" documents business processes, drawing on stakeholders, structures and objects defined in the Context and Object packages.

2.3 Use Case Model (Requirements)

A conceptual and high-level of defining "Cloud Computing" requirements is shown below (Figure 2). This model is an abstraction of models in requirements engineering and is used for the purpose of identifying different systems in and across any enterprise that needs to provide a CSB-based platform of computing resources.

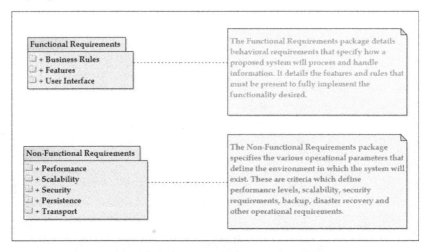

Figure 2: Fundamental Requirements Model

The idea behind capturing these use cases is to make explicit the services between systems in a complex landscape (such as used in enterprises or provider-based organizations for cloud computing). Another target is to have an architectural view of the project (cloud computing engagement and deployment) that can be checked against business process specifications.

Figure 3 (shown below) provides an abstraction of what the possible set of use cases will be at a fairly high-level. All the use cases are shown as invoking different types of systems. These systems can range from operating environments, hardware, platforms, networks, software, applications, databases, servers and all combinations of infrastructure. The important concept behind the use case model in Figure 3 is to show that use cases for a cloud computing environment are all about capturing requirements as a set that "emulates" or "simulates" an enterprise system usage. The enterprise system in this model is meant to reference any combination of services that will be part of the CSB.

Multiple users can be accessing the CSB. Hence, managing the access of resources (systems in Figure 3) will be captured. Any type of usage by the various users can be depicted but Figure 3 is meant to show that use cases will drive what is needed or demanded by different types of users.

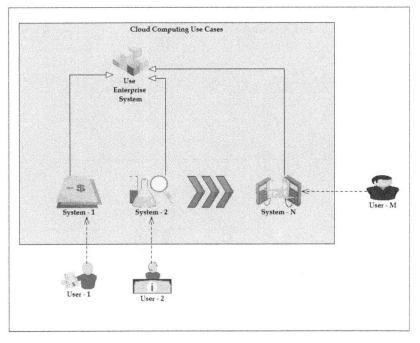

Figure 3: Use Case Model

2.4 Sequence Model (Scenarios)

The next stage is to examine the dynamic behavior of the system using scenarios. UML sequence diagrams are the natural mechanism for this. Modeling the sequence diagrams verifies the relationships and interfaces that are captured in package diagrams (for each functionality or process of the CSB) and will also identify gaps (if any) in the design. Usually, these gaps are the parts that require manual intervention (a.k.a. human intervention) by the system integrators or designers. The design of these features can use traditional UML techniques, albeit constrained by the existing structure imposed by the packages being used in the overall CSB system.

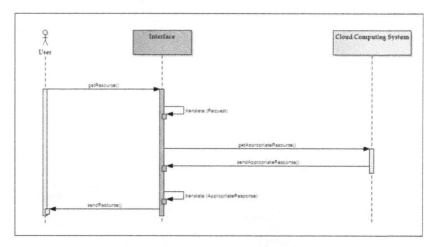

Figure 4: Sequence Model – Abstract View

2.5 Component Model

The physical aspects of the design, as well as the interfaces between the components, vis-à-vis CSB can be represented using component and deployment diagrams. The key factor to note is that, in CSB deployment, everything is "programmable" through appropriate "interfaces". These interfaces can be special "API" ("Application Programmable Interface") type components (modules) that will help in connecting users to the entire CSB infrastructure, platforms, software and other facets.

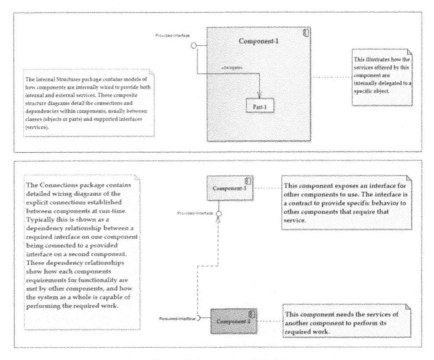

Figure 5: Component Model

2.6 Deployment Model

UML deployment diagrams can be used to document the physical aspects of any CSB project and to identify the interfaces between the packages. However, CSB as well as cloud computing will usually include a deeper level of design involving synchronizing of data between the systems and implementing end-to-end business processes covering all of the packages in a single-use case. UML helps in capturing all dimensions of the deployment model and these are listed below for completeness.

The deployment model will cover at least some of the following (or more) components in a CSB.

- Virtual machines as the standard deployment objects. This means that the hardware is abstracted and is horizontally scalable to address user needs on a very high performance and extremely efficient time basis.
- It is like having an infinite capacity of resources where everything is loosely coupled so much so that applications can be deployed independently of how servers are used.
- Common interfaces between providers (agencies) and users as well as developers, administrators, systems engineers and a host of other professionals.

- Virtual appliances can include servers, database appliances, network hardware, firmware and other things that are typically found in any data center.

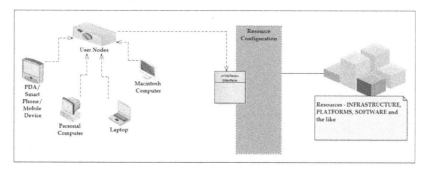

Figure 6: Deployment Model

The model will capture all types of user nodes (as shown in Figure 6). The extensions of user nodes are depicted as shown but there can be many more possibilities of new devices to be considered.

2.7 CSB Model Driven Architecture

Figure 7 is a depiction of a sample high-level actionable architecture for CSB. This diagram shows that cloud computing is built on a foundation of the CSB and all resources will be captured as services. These services are essentially a collection of every facet that is needed for any user to be able to work in a computing environment that facilitates a total virtualization of everyday work. Instead of being forced to buy or rent expensive equipment as well as all associated software, users can now use the services provided by agencies (organizations, providers and the like) for all computing needs. The responsibility of managing user needs is passed on to the agencies (organizations, providers and the like) and the users will not have to reckon with issues around functional as well as quality (non-functional) needs because they will pay for fault-tolerant services as they do for any other type of utility. This is what the true value of cloud computing is all about.

From today's world of multifarious web applications or systems, users will move to using everything through IaaS, PaaS, SaaS and a whole range of combinations to seamlessly work with what they need. Since all these services are paid for by the users, the onus of providing high quality services is passed on to providers. Therefore, organizations can create private, public or hybrid combinations for cloud computing for any type of user base without operational or physical complexities that prevail in traditional web computing environments of today. Even bandwidth provisioning can be done as a service manifestation so that the users will not be constrained as in today's web infrastructure. The truest gain of cloud computing viability revolves around bandwidth power for users (handled for all user bases through "bandwidth services") which is why CSB provides the correct architectural model to drive cloud computing to a great success.

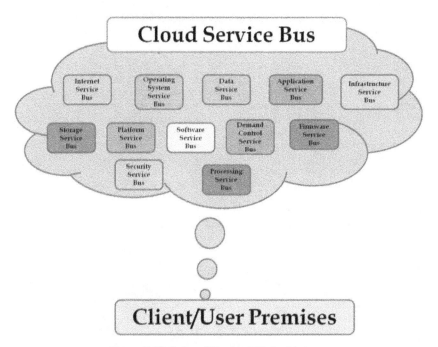

Figure 7: High-Level Target CSB Architecture

3. Conclusion

The "summum bonum" of this paper has been to show the feasibility of the CSB as the actionable architecture for practical cloud computing. This paper is not intended to be any form of treatise but rather to demonstrate the viability of an architectural perspective of cloud computing. The purposeful conclusion of this paper has been to reach a logical goal of showing that cloud computing is really a superset of web and internet-based applications, through a CSB architecture, that covers the whole spectrum of infrastructure, platforms, software and much more to make user experiences move to a virtualized environment with physical manifestations that are executable through a network-driven approach.

As many experts have suggested, the "pay-per-use solution" of cloud computing obviously makes sense if the unit cost of cloud services is lower than dedicated/owned capacity. In actuality, cloud computing does provide this cost advantage. However, a pure cloud solution also makes sense even if its unit cost is higher, as long as the "peak-to-average" ratio of the demand curve is higher than the cost differential between on-demand and dedicated capacity. In other words, even if cloud services cost, for example, twice as much, a pure cloud solution makes sense for those demand curves where the "peak-to-average" ratio is two-to-one or higher. This is very often the case across a variety of industries. The reason for this is that the fixed capacity dedicated solution must be built to peak, whereas the cost of the on-demand pay-per-use solution is proportional to the average.

It is also imperative to note that leveraging pay-per-use pricing, either in a wholly on-demand solution or a hybrid with dedicated capacity turns out to make sense any time there is a peak of "short enough" duration. Specifically, if the percentage of time spent at peak is less than the inverse of the utility premium, using a cloud computing environment or other pay-per-use utility for at least part of the solution makes practical sense. For example, even if the cost of cloud services were, say, four times as much as owned capacity, they still make sense as part of the solution if peak demand only occurs one-quarter of the time or less. All of this proves the efficacy and business value proposition for providers and users vis-à-vis cloud computing. We are at the threshold of creating an environment of the best user experience through cloud computing and providers can leverage the MDA (model driven architecture) principles to provide the most optimal solutions vis-à-vis cloud computing for all types of users.

4. References

[1] K. Mukherjee and G. Sahoo [International Conference on Advances in Computing, Control and Telecommunication Technologies - 2009 IEEE Publication].
[2] Joe Weinman in ["Mathematical Proof of the Inevitability of Cloud Computing" – Cloudonomics, November 2009]
More publications and articles by Joe Weinman are available at:
  • http://www.joeweinman.com/Papers.htm
  • http://www.complexmodels.com/
[3] Peter Fingar [Enterprise Cloud Computing – published book].
[4] Sun Microsystems, Inc. – "The Network is the computer" paradigm and associated deployment papers like "Introduction to Cloud Computing Architecture" and "Take your business to a higher level" series of June 2009.
[5] IBM Cloud Computing papers in IBM Smart Business portfolio.
[6] Microsoft Cloud Computing papers in ACM Symposium on Cloud Computing 2010 [ACM SOCC 2010].

5. Citations

  • **All the diagrams have been created from a UML modeling tool called Enterprise Architect (http://www.sparxsystems.com/) and some adaptations have been made (with appropriate customizations) for this paper.**
  • **Ideas have been adopted form major corporations like Sun Microsystems, IBM and Microsoft vis-à-vis the directions of cloud computing so as make the presentation of the paper more holistic.**
  • **References cited are not just academic work but are taken from actual work done in real deployment environments.**

6. Acknowledgements

I am extremely grateful to all my colleagues in Infosys for encouraging me to publish this paper. I am overjoyed to share my experience and will have the opportunity to interact with professionals who are extremely talented in leading-edge topics that will help our clients and company.